Kids' Ideas
with frozen dough

Rhodes Bake-N-Serv™
Salt Lake City, Utah

Editors:　　　　　　　　　　Madelynne Brown
　　　　　　　　　　　　　　Jenna Jackson
　　　　　　　　　　　　　　Sue Petersen

Background Illustration
　& Design:　　　　　　　　Madelynne Brown
Recipe Illustration:　　　　Robyn Reading
Photography:　　　　　　　Mitch Rogers, Dave Wheeler, Bill Mitchell
Art Director:　　　　　　　Dane Beck
Sculpture Creation:　　　　Zoe Ann Farnsworth, Jenna Jackson,
　　　　　　　　　　　　　　Sue Petersen, Robyn Reading

A special thanks to all of the Rhodes Bake-N-Serv
employees and customers.

All of us at Rhodes Bake-N-Serv are dedicated to providing
you with fun and family-oriented ideas for home baking.

We appreciate your comments and suggestions. Write to
us at Rhodes Bake-N-Serv Recipes, P.O. Box 25487, Salt
Lake City, UT 84125.

If you would like to order additional copies of this book,
please call our toll-free Bake Line: 1-800-876-7333, or visit
our internet site:

www.rhodesbread.com

Pictured on front cover: Baby 'Gator (recipe on pages 46-47)
Pictured on back cover: Dough Writing (recipe on pages 74-75)
Pictured on these pages: Ken Farnsworth and grandchildren: Hans, Benjamin and Stefan Lehnardt

Foreword

For years, we've been collecting fun creative baking ideas and have put some of our best into this book! Remember, at Rhodes we not only guarantee our product, we also guarantee you'll have fun using it. I hope these recipes bring you the same joy I've had with my children and grandchildren.

Ken

Ken Farnsworth, Jr.
Rhodes Bake-N-Serv

Rhodes
NO-FAULT
GUARANTEE
SINCE 1958
Bake-N-Serv™

What YOU Car

Frosty
Pages 6-7

Mittens
Pages 8-9

Fantastic Football
Pages 10-11

Cloverleaf Rolls
Pages 12-13

Lullaby Lamb
Pages 14-15

Tasty Tulip
Pages 16-17

Bunny
Pages 18-19

Freddy Frog
Pages 20-21

Lucky Duck
Pages 22-23

Lil' Chicks
Pages 24-25

Easter Egg Nest
Pages 26-27

Baked Bread
Pages 30-31

Caterpillar
Pages 32-33

Flounder
Pages 34-35

Starfish
Pages 36-37

Jam Bellies
Pages 38-39

Crusty Crab
Pages 40-41

Sallee's Seashell
Pages 42-43

French Toast
Pages 44-45

Baby 'Gator
Pages 46-47

Betty Butterfly
Pages 48-49

Lulu Lady Bug
Pages 52-53

Darling Daisy
Pages 54-55

My Personal Pizza
Pages 56-57

Make and Bake!

Waffle Wiggles
Pages 58-59

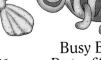
Trout
Pages 60-61

Busy Bee
Pages 62-63

Fruit Pizza
Pages 64-65

Dough-Dino
Pages 66-67

Soft Pretzels
Pages 70-71

Tommy Turtle
Pages 72-73

Dough Writing
Pages 74-75

Piggy
Pages 76-77

A+ Apples
Pages 78-79

Breadsticks
Pages 80-81

Autumn Leaves
Pages 82-83

Curly Dogs
Pages 84-85

Spooky Spider
Pages 86-87

Ghost
Pages 88-89

Witch's Cat
Pages 92-93

Barney the Bat
Pages 94-95

Cinnamon Rolls
Pages 96-97

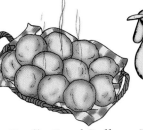
Really Good Rolls
Pages 98-99

Texas Turkey
Pages 100-101

Honey Bear
Pages 102-103

Maddie Mouse
Pages 104-105

Moose
Pages 106-107

Tall Timbers
Pages 108-109

Frosty

...the doughman

Equipment
cookie sheet
non-stick cooking spray
knife
hot pads

Ingredients
8 Rhodes Texas™ rolls
2 mini-kisses
   honey
    2 pretzel sticks

Advance Preparation
Put the frozen rolls in a plastic bag. Leave them in the refrigerator overnight or on the counter for about 2 hours, until thawed but still cold.

1. Spray the cookie sheet.

2. Flatten 3 rolls together for the bottom of the snowman and 2 rolls for the middle. Cut 1 roll in half, and make the head with 1-1/2 rolls. Put them on the cookie sheet.

3. Cut a smile and pull it open.

4. Roll the other half roll into a rope. Flatten it and put it above the head for the brim of the hat.

5. Flatten the last roll into a rectangle for the hat. Put it above the brim. Cut a piece off the bottom for the hat band. Leave it in place.

6. Turn the oven on to 350°F. Wait 20 minutes.

7. Just before baking, open the mouth again. Bake the snowman about 20 minutes. Turn the oven off. With the hot pads, remove the cookie sheet from the oven and let it cool.

8. Stick the mini-kisses on the face with some honey for the eyes. Push the pretzels into the middle section for the arms.

See instructions for the mittens on pages 8 & 9.

7

Mittens

Equipment
cookie sheet
non-stick cooking spray
knife
hot pads

Burr! It's cold...

Ingredients
4 Rhodes Texas™ rolls

Advance Preparation
Put the frozen rolls in a plastic bag.
Leave them in the refrigerator overnight
or on the counter for about 2 hours, until
thawed but still cold.

8

1. Spray the cookie sheet.

2. Flatten 2 rolls together to make the mitten. Put it on the cookie sheet.

3. Cut a strip off the bottom for the wrist band. Flatten it and put it below the mitten.

4. Make a big cut in the side of the mitten for the thumb. Pull the piece down.

5. Make another mitten.

6. Turn the oven on to 350°F. Wait 20 minutes.

7. Bake the mittens about 20 minutes. Turn the oven off. With the hot pads, remove the cookie sheet from the oven and let it cool. Makes 2 sandwich size mittens.

For Small Mittens to Fit on the Snowman

Use 1/2 roll for each mitten. When the mittens have baked and cooled, insert the pretzel sticks for the arms.

Fan-tastic Football

Equipment
cookie sheet
non-stick cooking spray
knife
toothpick
hot pads

Ingredients
3 Rhodes Texas™ rolls

Advance Preparation
Put the frozen rolls in a plastic bag. Leave them in the refrigerator overnight or on the counter for about 2 hours, until thawed but still cold.

1. Spray the cookie sheet.

2. Flatten 2 rolls together to make the football. Put it on the cookie sheet.

3. Cut 1 roll in half. Put 1 half under the football to make the middle higher.

4. Roll the other half into a rope for the laces. Cut it into 4 pieces.

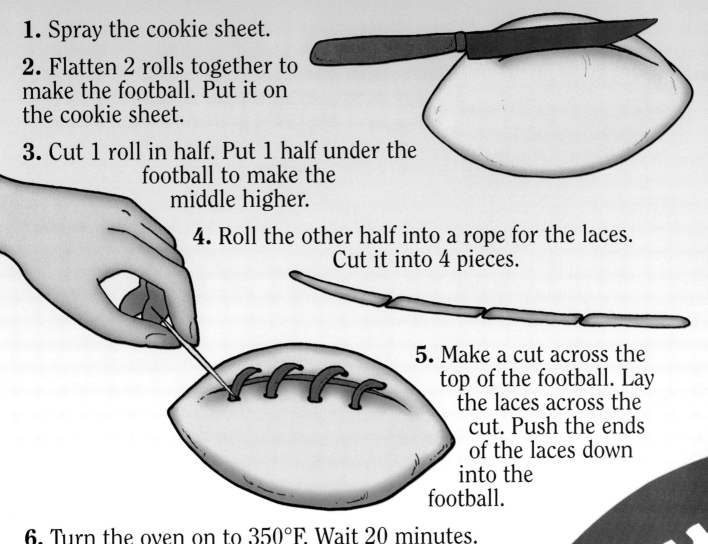

5. Make a cut across the top of the football. Lay the laces across the cut. Push the ends of the laces down into the football.

6. Turn the oven on to 350°F. Wait 20 minutes.

7. Bake the football about 20 minutes. Turn the oven off. With the hot pads, remove the cookie sheet from the oven and let it cool.

Touchdown!

11

Cloverleaf Rolls

Equipment
muffin tin
non-stick
  cooking spray
scissors
plastic wrap
hot pads

Ingredients
9 Rhodes™ rolls

Advance Preparation
Put the frozen rolls in a plastic bag. Leave them in the refrigerator overnight or on the counter for about 2 hours, until thawed but still cold.

1. Spray the muffin tin.

2. Cut each roll in half. Put 3 halves into each muffin cup.

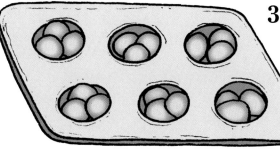

3. Spray a piece of plastic wrap and cover the rolls loosely. Let the rolls rise about 2 hours or until they are twice as big.

4. Turn the oven on to 350°F. Wait until it is hot!

5. Carefully remove the plastic wrap. Bake the rolls 15 to 20 minutes or until they are light golden brown.

6. Turn the oven off. With the hot pads, remove the muffin tin from the oven. Tip the rolls out and let them cool slightly.

Good Luck!

Lullaby Lamb

Equipment
cookie sheet
non-stick
   cooking spray
scissors
bowl
fork
pastry brush
hot pads

Ingredients
15 Rhodes™ rolls
1 raisin
1 egg
sesame seeds or poppy seeds

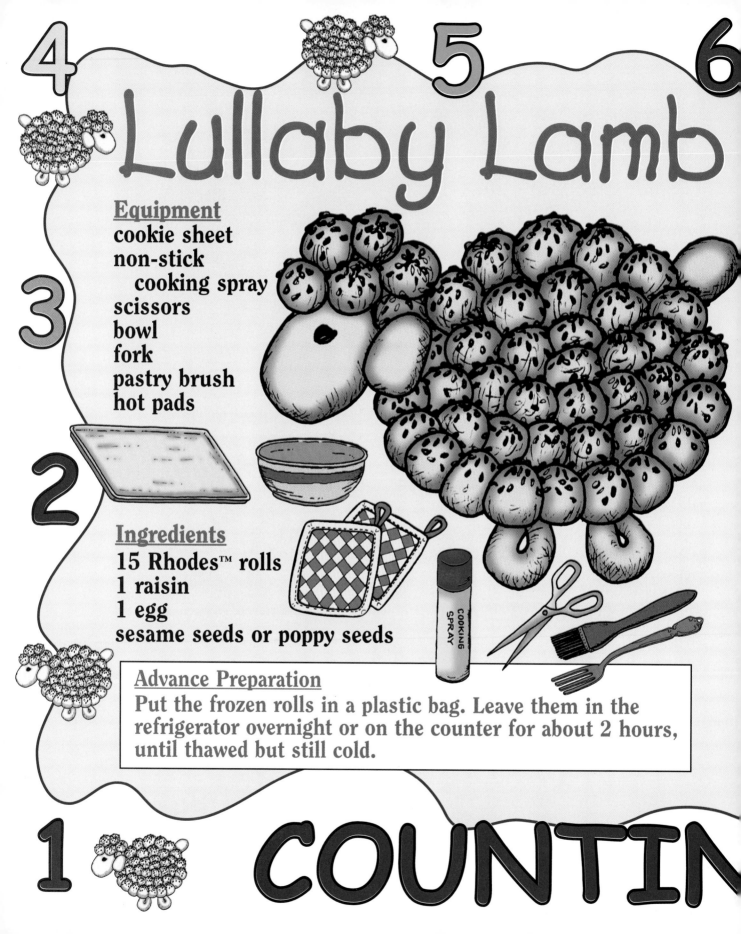

Advance Preparation
Put the frozen rolls in a plastic bag. Leave them in the refrigerator overnight or on the counter for about 2 hours, until thawed but still cold.

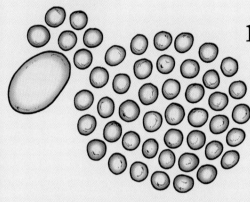

1. Spray the cookie sheet.

2. Flatten 1 roll into an oval for the face. Put it on the cookie sheet.

3. Cut 12 rolls into 4 pieces each. Put them on the cookie sheet for the body and the top of the head.

4. Use 1 roll to make the ear and the tail. Put them on the lamb.

5. With the last roll make the feet. Put them in place.

6. Beat the egg and brush it on the lamb. Push the raisin on the head for the eye. Sprinkle with the seeds—try not to get any on the face, tail or feet.

7. Turn the oven on to 350°F. Wait 30 minutes.

8. Bake the lamb about 20 minutes. Turn the oven off. With the hot pads, remove the cookie sheet from the oven and let it cool.

G SHEEP

Baaa! Baaa!

Tasty Tulip

Equipment
cookie sheet
non-stick cooking spray
scissors
hot pads

Ingredients
2 Rhodes Texas™ rolls

Advance Preparation
Put the frozen rolls in a plastic bag. Leave them in the refrigerator overnight or on the counter for about 2 hours, until thawed but still cold.

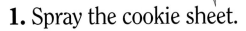

1. Spray the cookie sheet.

2. Flatten 1 roll into the tulip. Cut out 2 triangles. Put the tulip on the cookie sheet.

3. Squish the cut-out pieces together and roll them into a stem. Put 1 end under the tulip.

4. Cut the other roll almost in half for the leaves. Flatten and spread the leaves apart. Put it at the bottom of the stem.

5. Turn the oven on to 350°F. Wait 15 minutes.

6. Bake the tulip about 15 minutes. Turn the oven off. With the hot pads, remove the cookie sheet from the oven and let it cool.

To Display: Glue a short dowel or pencil to the back of each tulip, leaving about 2-inches sticking out at the bottom of each flower. Fill a planter with styrafoam. Push the dowel or pencil into the foam. Hide the foam with some fake grass.

Bunny

Equipment
cookie sheet
non-stick cooking spray
scissors
hot pads

Ingredients
5 Rhodes Texas™ rolls
2 sliced almonds
2 raisins

Advance Preparation
Put the frozen rolls in a plastic bag. Leave them in the refrigerator overnight or on the counter for about 2 hours, until thawed but still cold.

1. Spray the cookie sheet.

2. Flatten 2 rolls together for the body. Put it on the cookie sheet.

3. Flatten 1 roll for the head. Put it above the body and cut the whiskers.

4. Pinch a small piece off 1 roll to make 2 cheeks and a nose. Put them on the face.

5. Cut the rest of the roll in half and make 2 ropes. Put them above the head for the ears and pinch the tops together.

6. Make the last roll into 2 large feet and 2 hands. Cut the fingers and toes. Put them by the bunny.

7. Push the raisins and almonds on the face for the eyes and teeth.

8. Turn the oven on to 350°F. Wait 20 minutes.

9. Bake the bunny about 20 minutes. Turn the oven off. With the hot pads, remove the cookie sheet from the oven and let it cool.

Freddy Frog

Equipment
cookie sheet
non-stick cooking spray
scissors
knife
hot pads

Ingredients
5 Rhodes Texas™ rolls

Advance Preparation
Put the frozen rolls in a plastic bag. Leave them in the refrigerator overnight or on the counter for about 2 hours, until thawed but still cold.

Ribbit! Ribbit!

1. Spray the cookie sheet.

2. Flatten 2 rolls together for the body. Put it on the cookie sheet.

3. Cut 1 roll in half and flatten each half to make the legs. Put them next to the body.

4. Cut another roll in half and make 2 feet. Clip the toes. Put the feet below the frog.

5. Cut the last roll into 3 pieces. Make 2 of the pieces into arms. Cut the fingers. Put the arms on the frog.

6. Use the last piece for 2 eye sockets and 2 eyes. Press your thumb deep into the eye sockets. Put them above the frog's head. Put the eyes in the sockets.

7. Cut a big smile.

8. Turn the oven on to 350°F. Wait 20 minutes.

9. Bake the frog about 20 minutes. Turn the oven off. With the hot pads, remove the cookie sheet from the oven and let it cool.

21

Lucky Duck

Equipment
cookie sheet
non-stick cooking spray
knife
hot pads

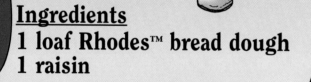

Ingredients
1 loaf Rhodes™ bread dough
1 raisin

Advance Preparation
Put the frozen rolls in a plastic bag. Leave them in the refrigerator overnight or on the counter for about 2 hours, until thawed but still cold.

1. Spray the cookie sheet.

2. Cut a small piece off the loaf. Flatten the rest of the loaf into the body, head and bill. Put it on the cookie sheet.

3. Cut the mouth open. Cut the bill off, but leave it in place.

4. Cut the tail feathers.

5. With the small piece of dough, make a wing, legs, and feet. Cut feathers on the wing, and toes on the feet. Put them all in place.

6. Push the raisin on the head for the eye. Turn the oven on to 350°F. Wait 20 minutes.

7. Bake the duck about 20 minutes. Turn the oven off. With the hot pads, remove the cookie sheet from the oven and let it cool.

Quack! Quack! Quack! Quack! Quack! Quack!

23

'Lil Chicks

Peep! Peep! Peep!

Equipment
cookie sheet
non-stick cooking spray
scissors
hot pads

COOKING SPRAY

Ingredients
2 Rhodes Texas™ roll
2 raisins

Advance Preparation
Put the frozen rolls in a plastic bag. Leave them in the refrigerator overnight or on the counter for about 2 hours, until thawed but still cold.

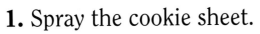

1. Spray the cookie sheet.

2. Flatten 1 roll for the body. Put it on the cookie sheet.

3. Flatten the other roll into a half circle for the egg shell. Cut out jagged triangles. Put the shell on the body.

4. Make a cone for the beak out of some leftover dough. Cut it open and put it on the chick.

5. Push the raisins on the face for the eyes.

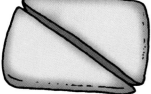

6. Using the rest of the leftover dough, make a rectangle. Cut it from corner to corner to make 2 wings. Cut the feathers and put the wings by the chick.

7. Turn the oven on to 350°F. Wait 15 minutes.

8. Bake the chick about 20 minutes. Turn the oven off. With the hot pads, remove the cookie sheet from the oven and let it cool.

Easter Egg Nest

Equipment
cookie sheet
non-stick cooking spray
scissors
hot pads

Ingredients
3 Rhodes Texas™ rolls
1 raw egg

Advance Preparation
Put the frozen rolls in a plastic bag. Leave them in the refrigerator overnight or on the counter for about 2 hours, until thawed but still cold.

1. Spray the cookie sheet.

2. Flatten each roll into a circle.

3. Make cuts around the outside of each circle.

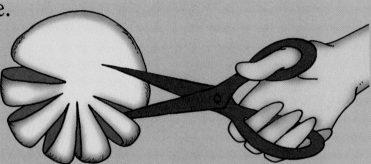

4. Stack the circles on top of each other. Put them on the cookie sheet.

5. Tangle some of the pieces around each other to look like straw.

6. Gently press the egg into the center of the nest.

7. Turn the oven on to 350°F. Wait 20 minutes.

8. Bake the egg nest about 20 minutes. Turn the oven off. With the hot pads, remove the cookie sheet from the oven and let it cool.

You can eat the egg.

Baked Bread

Equipment
loaf pan
non-stick cooking spray
plastic wrap
hot pads

Ingredients
1 loaf Rhodes™ bread dough

Advance Preparation
This recipe uses dough that is still frozen. After step 3, it can be put in the refrigerator overnight to thaw. Then let it rise 3 hours on the counter before following step 5.

the oven!

1. Spray the loaf pan.

2. Put the bread in the pan.

3. Spray the plastic wrap and cover the bread loosely.

4. Let the bread rise about 6 hours or until it is twice as big.

5. Turn the oven on to 350°F. Wait until it is hot!

6. Carefully remove the plastic wrap. Bake the bread for 25 minutes.

7. Turn the oven off. With the hot pads, remove the loaf pan from the oven. Remove the bread from the pan by tipping it out. Let the bread cool on its side.

1st Place

Caterpillar

Creepy, Crawly.

Equipment
cookie sheet
non-stick cooking spray
knife
hot pads

COOKING SPRAY

Ingredients
2 Rhodes Texas™ rolls

Advance Preparation
Put the frozen rolls in a plastic bag. Leave them in the refrigerator overnight or on the counter for about 2 hours, until thawed but still cold.

32

1. Spray the cookie sheet.

2. Cut 1 roll in half. Squish 1-1/2 rolls into a fat body. Put it on the cookie sheet.

3. Cut the head off. Leave it in place. Make cuts on the body.

4. Pinch 2 eyes off the last half and put them on the head.

5. Roll the rest of the dough into a rope and cut 10 legs. Put them in place.

6. Turn the oven on to 350°F. Wait 15 minutes.

7. Bake the caterpillar for about 20 minutes. Turn the oven off. With the hot pads, remove the cookie sheet from the oven and let it cool.

Hurry! before he crawls away!

33

Flounder

Equipment
cookie sheet
non-stick cooking spray
knife
hot pads

Ingredients
4 Rhodes Texas™ rolls

Don't put me in the bathtub!

Advance Preparation
Put the frozen rolls in a plastic bag. Leave them in the refrigerator overnight or on the counter for about 2 hours, until thawed but still cold.

1. Spray the cookie sheet.

2. Flatten 2 rolls together for the body. Put it on the cookie sheet.

3. Cut another roll in half. Flatten each half for the tail fins. Put them by the body.

4. Use the last roll to make the eye socket, the eye, the mouth, the lower fin and the top fin. Cut some jagged pieces out of the top fin. Put all the pieces, except the eye and socket, in place.

5. Press your thumb deep into the mouth and eye socket. Put the eye in the socket and put it on the flounder.

6. Cut 3 wavy lines on the body.

7. Turn the oven on to 350°F. Wait 20 minutes.

8. Push your thumb into the mouth again just before baking. Bake the flounder about 20 minutes. Turn the oven off. With the hot pads, remove the cookie sheet from the oven and let it cool.

What a catch!

StarFish

Equipment
cookie sheet
non-stick cooking spray
scissors
hot pads

Ingredients
5 Rhodes Texas™ rolls

Advance Preparation
Put the frozen rolls in a plastic bag. Leave them in the refrigerator overnight or on the counter for about 2 hours, until thawed but still cold.

36

1. Spray the cookie sheet.

2. Cut the rolls in half and flatten them.

3. Put 5 pieces on the cookie sheet to make a star — not too close together! Pinch the tips.

4. Make another starfish.

5. Turn the oven on to 350°F. Wait 20 minutes.

6. Bake the starfish about 20 minutes. Turn the oven off. With the hot pads, remove the cookie sheet from the oven and let it cool.

Make a wish

Jam Bellies

Strawberries • Strawberries • Strawberries • Strawberries •

Equipment
cookie sheet
non-stick cooking spray
plastic wrap
fork
small bowl
hot pads
pastry brush
spatula
spoon

Ingredients
6 Rhodes Texas™ rolls
6 tablespoons strawberry jam
1 cup powdered sugar
1 tablespoon soft butter
1/2 teaspoon vanilla extract
2-3 tablespoons milk

Advance Preparation
Put the frozen rolls in a plastic bag. Leave them in the refrigerator overnight or on the counter for about 2 hours, until thawed but still cold.

38

1. Spray the cookie sheet.

2. Flatten each roll into a circle. Put them on the cookie sheet.

3. Spray the plastic wrap and cover the rolls loosely.

4. Let the rolls rise about 2 hours or until they are twice as big.

5. Turn the oven on to 350°F. Carefully remove the plastic wrap.

6. Push down the center of each roll to make a dip. Fill it with a tablespoon of jam.

7. Bake the jam bellies about 20 minutes. While they are baking, mix together the powdered sugar, butter, vanilla and milk.

8. Turn the oven off. With the hot pads, remove the cookie sheet from the oven. Take the jam bellies off the pan. Brush them lightly with the icing while they are still warm.

9. After the jam bellies have cooled, drizzle the rest of the icing over the tops.

Crusty Crab

Equipment
cookie sheet
non-stick cooking spray
knife
hot pads

Ingredients
5 Rhodes Texas Rolls

PINCH! PINCH!

Advance Preparation
Put the frozen rolls in a plastic bag. Leave them in the refrigerator overnight or on the counter for about 2 hours, until thawed but still cold.

1. Spray the cookie sheet.

2. Flatten 2 rolls together for the body. Put it on the cookie sheet.

3. Pinch a small piece of dough off 1 roll to make 2 small eyes. Put them on the body.

4. Cut the rest of the roll in half to make the arms. Put them by the body.

5. Cut another roll in half for the claws. Put them by the arms and slice them open.

6. Roll the last roll into a rope and cut 6 legs. Put them in place.

7. Turn the oven on to 350°F. Wait 20 minutes.

8. Bake the crab about 20 minutes. Turn the oven off. With the hot pads, remove the cookie sheet from the oven and let it cool.

Arm

Claw

41

Sallee's SeaShell

Equipment
cookie sheet
non-stick cooking spray
hot pads

COOKING SPRAY

Ingredients
2 Rhodes Texas™ rolls

Advance Preparation
Put the frozen rolls in a plastic bag. Leave them in
the refrigerator overnight or on the counter for
about 2 hours, until thawed but still cold.

42

1. Spray the cookie sheet.

2. Squish the rolls together. Roll them into a long rope.

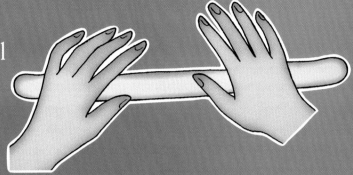

3. Swirl the rope on the cookie sheet. Tuck in the tip.

4. Turn the oven on to 350°F. Wait 20 minutes.

5. Bake the seashell about 20 minutes. Turn the oven off. With the hot pads, remove the cookie sheet from the oven and let it cool.

She sells seashells down by the seashore

43

French Toast

Equipment
shallow bowl
fork
large skillet or griddle
non-stick cooking spray
spatula

Ingredients
1 loaf Rhodes™ bread
4 eggs
1/4 cup milk
1/2 teaspoon vanilla
1/2 teaspoon cinnamon
1/8 teaspoon nutmeg
syrup or jam

Advance Preparation
Bake the bread dough according to the package directions the day before.

44

1. Beat the eggs until foamy. Add the milk, vanilla, cinnamon and nutmeg and beat again.

2. Put the skillet or griddle on the burner. Turn the burner on to medium heat. Spray the hot pan.

3. Cut the loaf into 8 slices. Dip 1 slice into the egg mixture and coat both sides. Put it on the pan.

4. Cook it until the bottom is golden brown, about 3 minutes. Turn it over and cook the other side.

5. Repeat steps 3 and 4 for the rest of the slices. Turn the burner off. Serve the toast warm with syrup or jam.

Ooh! La! La!

45

Baby 'Gator

You can eat me for lunch...

Equipment
cookie sheet
non-stick cooking spray
knife
aluminum foil
scissors
hot pads

COOKING SPRAY

ALUMINUM FOIL

Ingredients
1 loaf Rhodes™ bread dough

Advance Preparation
Put the frozen loaf in a plastic bag. Leave it in the refrigerator overnight or on the counter for about 3 hours, until thawed but still cold.

1. Spray the cookie sheet.

2. Cut a piece off the end of the loaf. Roll the rest of the loaf into a baseball bat. Put it on the cookie sheet. Flatten the big end into the gator's head.

3. Make cuts down each side of the gator. Pull them out to make 4 legs.

4. Cut a mouth. Hold it open with crinkled up foil. Pinch the end of the nose up.

5. With the rest of the dough, make 2 eyes and 4 feet. Cut the toes.

6. Put the eyes on the top of the head. Put the feet under the legs.

7. Clip the scales on the gator.

8. Turn the oven on to 350°F. Wait 20 minutes.

9. Bake the gator about 25 minutes. Turn the oven off. With the hot pads, remove the cookie sheet from the oven and let it cool. Take the foil out of the gator's mouth when it has cooled.

47

Betty Butterfly

Equipment
cookie sheet
non-stick cooking spray
scissors
hot pads

Flutter! Flutter! Flutter!

Ingredients
5 Rhodes Texas™ rolls

Advance Preparation
Put the frozen rolls in a plastic bag. Leave them in the refrigerator overnight or on the counter for about 2 hours, until thawed but still cold.

48

1. Spray the cookie sheet.

2. Cut 1 roll in half. Roll 1 half into a rope for the body. Put it on the cookie sheet. Save the other half.

3. Flatten 1 roll for each of the bottom wings. Put them next to the body.

4. Cut another roll in half and flatten the halves into 2 top wings. Put them in place.

5. With the last roll and a half make 2 small eyes, the antennae and shapes for the wings. Put them on the butterfly.

6. Turn the oven on to 350°F. Wait 20 minutes.

7. Bake the butterfly about 20 minutes. Turn the oven off. With the hot pads, remove the cookie sheet from the oven and let it cool.

How many designs can you think of for the wings?

49

Lulu Lady Bug

Equipment
cookie sheet
non-stick cooking spray
knife
hot pads

Ingredients
2 Rhodes Texas™ rolls

Advance Preparation
Put the frozen rolls in a plastic bag. Leave them in the refrigerator overnight or on the counter for about 2 hours, until thawed but still cold.

1. Spray the cookie sheet.

2. Flatten 1 roll into an oval for the body. Put it on the cookie sheet.

3. Cut 1/4 off the end for the head. Leave it in place. Cut lines for the wings.

4. Roll the other roll into a rope and cut it into 7 pieces. Make 6 of the pieces into legs. Put them in place.

5. Make the last piece into 8 balls for eyes and spots. Put them on the ladybug.

6. Turn the oven on to 350°F. Wait 20 minutes.

7. Bake the ladybug about 20 minutes. Turn the oven off. With the hot pads, remove the cookie sheet from the oven and let it cool.

Ladybug! Ladybug! Fly away home!

53

Darling Daisy

Equipment
cookie sheet
non-stick cooking spray
scissors
hot pads

Ingredients
4 Rhodes Texas™ rolls

Advance Preparation
Put the frozen rolls in a plastic bag. Leave them in the refrigerator overnight or on the counter for about 2 hours, until thawed but still cold.

1. Spray the cookie sheet.

2. Cut 3 rolls into 3 pieces each. Roll 1 piece into a ball for the center of the flower. Put it on the cookie sheet.

3. Roll another piece into a stem. Put it under the center.

4. Flatten the rest of the pieces into petals. Put them around the center of the flower.

5. Cut the last roll almost in half for the leaves. Flatten and spread the leaves apart. Put it at the bottom of the stem.

6. Turn the oven on to 350°F. Wait 20 minutes.

7. Bake the daisy about 20 minutes. Turn the oven off. With the hot pads, remove the cookie sheet from the oven and let it cool.

For a sweet center:
Just before baking, gently push the center of the flower down and fill it with jam.

My Personal Pizza

Equipment
non-stick cooking spray
cookie sheet
spatula
hot pads

COOKING SPRAY

Ingredients
2 Rhodes Texas™ rolls
pizza sauce
shredded cheese
your choice of pizza toppings

Advance Preparation
Put the frozen rolls in a plastic bag. Let them thaw at room temperature for 3 to 4 hours, or until soft and risen.

1. Spray the cookie sheet. Turn the oven on to 350°F.

2. Flatten 2 rolls together for the pizza crust. Put it on the cookie sheet.

3. Pinch the sides up to make an edge. Spread the sauce on the pizza.

4. Sprinkle the cheese on your pizza. Put on your choice of toppings.

5. Bake the pizza about 15 minutes, or until the cheese is bubbly. Turn the oven off. With the hot pads, remove the cookie sheet from the oven and let it cool slightly.

Let's have a pizza party!

Waffle Wiggles

Equipment
waffle iron
non-stick cooking spray
fork

Ingredients
12 Rhodes™ Texas rolls
butter, peanut butter, jam, honey, syrup
  or powdered sugar, if desired

Advance Preparation
Put the frozen rolls in a plastic bag. Let them thaw at room temperature for 3 to 4 hours, or until soft and risen.

1. Turn the waffle iron on high.

2. Flatten each roll into a big circle.

3. Spray the waffle iron. Put a flattened roll in the middle of the waffle iron and close the lid.

4. Cook the waffle wiggle about 45 seconds or until light golden brown.

5. Remove the waffle with a fork—it will be HOT!

6. Repeat with the rest of the rolls. Turn the waffle iron off. Serve the waffle wiggles warm.

FOR BREAKFAST:
Spread with butter and sprinkle with powdered sugar. Top with syrup.

FOR A SNACK:
Spread with peanut butter and jam or honey.

Trout

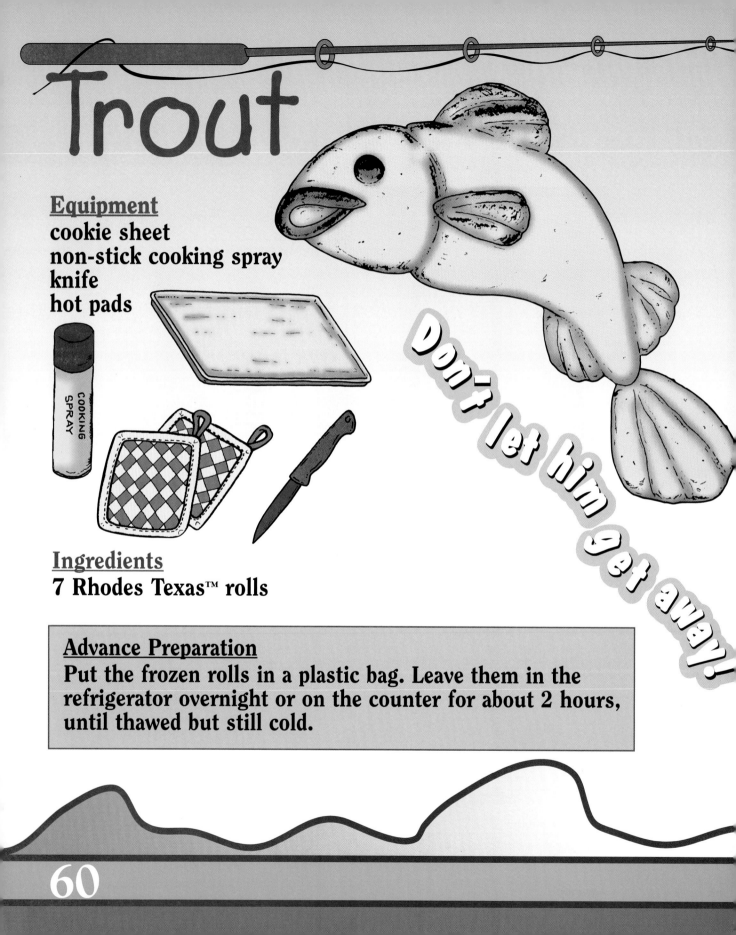

Equipment
cookie sheet
non-stick cooking spray
knife
hot pads

Ingredients
7 Rhodes Texas™ rolls

Don't let him get away!

Advance Preparation
Put the frozen rolls in a plastic bag. Leave them in the refrigerator overnight or on the counter for about 2 hours, until thawed but still cold.

1. Spray the cookie sheet.

2. Flatten 3 rolls together for the body. Put it on the cookie sheet. Curve the tail.

3. Press 2 rolls together for the head. Put it next to the body.

4. Cut 1 roll into 4 pieces. Make 4 small fins. Put them in place.

5. With the last roll make a long tail fin, an eye and the lips and put them on the trout.

6. Make cuts on each fin. Press your finger deep into the trout's mouth.

7. Turn the oven on to 350°F. Wait 20 minutes.

8. Bake the trout about 20 minutes. Turn the oven off. With the hot pads, remove the cookie sheet from the oven and let it cool.

Gone Fishin'

Busy Bee

Ingredients
cookie sheet
non-stick cooking spray
knife
hot pads

Ingredients
4 Rhodes Texas™ rolls

BZZZZZ
BZZZZZ

Advance Preparation
Put the frozen rolls in a plastic bag.
Leave them in the refrigerator
overnight or on the counter for about 2
hours, until thawed but still cold.

1. Spray the cookie sheet.

2. Flatten 2 rolls together to make the body. Put it on the cookie sheet.

3. Make cuts on the body and pinch the stinger.

4. Cut 1 roll in half. Flatten 1 half for the head. Put it by the body.

5. With the other half, make 3 legs, the antennae and eyes. Put them in place.

6. Cut a large smile in the face.

7. Cut the last roll in half and flatten both halves to make 2 wings. Cut criss-cross designs on each wing. Put them on the bee.

8. Turn the oven on to 350°F. Wait 20 minutes.

9. Bake the bee about 20 minutes. Turn the oven off. With the hot pads, remove the cookie sheet from the oven and let it cool.

Fruit Pizza

Equipment
12-inch pizza pan
non-stick cooking spray
rolling pin
fork
knife
hot pads

Ingredients
6 Rhodes Texas™ rolls
fruit flavored cream cheese
sliced fruit

Advance Preparation
Put the frozen rolls in a plastic bag. Let them thaw at room temperature for 3 to 4 hours, or until soft and risen.

1. Spray the pizza pan. Turn the oven on to 350°F.

2. Press the rolls into a ball and roll them into a crust to fit the pizza pan. Put the crust on the pan.

3. Poke holes in the crust to keep it from bubbling.

4. Bake the crust about 15 minutes. Turn the oven off. With the hot pads, remove the pan from the oven and let it cool completely.

5. Spread the crust with the cream cheese.

6. Arrange the fruit on top.

This is one pizza you'll want to eat cold!

65

Dough-Dino

It's an Earthshake!

Equipment
cookie sheet
non-stick cooking spray
knife
scissors
hot pads

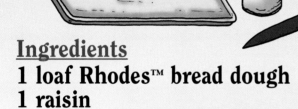

Ingredients
1 loaf Rhodes™ bread dough
1 raisin

Advance Preparation
Put the frozen loaf in a plastic bag.
Leave it in the refrigerator overnight or on
the counter for about 3 hours, until
thawed but still cold.

1. Spray the cookie sheet.

2. Cut a small piece off the loaf. Roll it into the tail and set it aside.

3. Flatten the rest of the loaf into the dinosaur's body. Put it on the cookie sheet.

4. Cut a square out of the body and take it off the cookie sheet.

5. Cut the legs and pull them apart. Clip the toes.

6. Make a long neck and head out of the square of dough. Put it by the body. Cut the mouth.

7. Put the tail on.

8. Push the raisin on the head for the eye. Turn the oven on to 350°F. Wait 30 minutes.

9. Bake the dinosaur about 25 minutes. Turn the oven off. With the hot pads, remove the cookie sheet from the oven and let it cool.

Dough-Dino
see recipe on pages 66 & 67

Soft Pretzels

Equipment
cookie sheet
non-stick cooking spray
knife
hot pads

Ingredients
1 loaf Rhodes™ bread dough
melted butter
cinnamon and sugar

Advance Preparation
Put the frozen loaf in a plastic bag. Leave it in the
refrigerator overnight or on the counter for about
3 hours, until thawed but still cold.

1. Spray the cookie sheet.

2. Cut the loaf lengthwise into 8 long strips. Roll each strip into a long rope.

3. Make 8 double twisted pretzels. Put them on the cookie sheet about 2 inches apart.

4. Spray the plastic wrap and cover the pretzels loosely. Let them rise about 45 minutes.

5. Turn the oven on to 350°F. Wait until the oven is hot!

6. Carefully remove the plastic wrap. Bake the pretzels about 20 minutes. Turn the oven off. With the hot pads, remove the cookie sheet from the oven.

7. Dip the pretzels in the melted butter while still warm. Sprinkle with cinnamon and sugar. Serve them warm with a glass of milk.

Tommy Turtle

For a great lunch hollow out the shell and fill it with your favorite salad!

Equipment
cookie sheet
non-stick cooking spray
scissors
aluminum foil
hot pads

Ingredients
7 Rhodes Texas™ rolls
2 small raisins

Advance Preparation
Put the frozen rolls in a plastic bag. Leave them in the refrigerator overnight or on the counter for about 2 hours, until thawed but still cold.

72

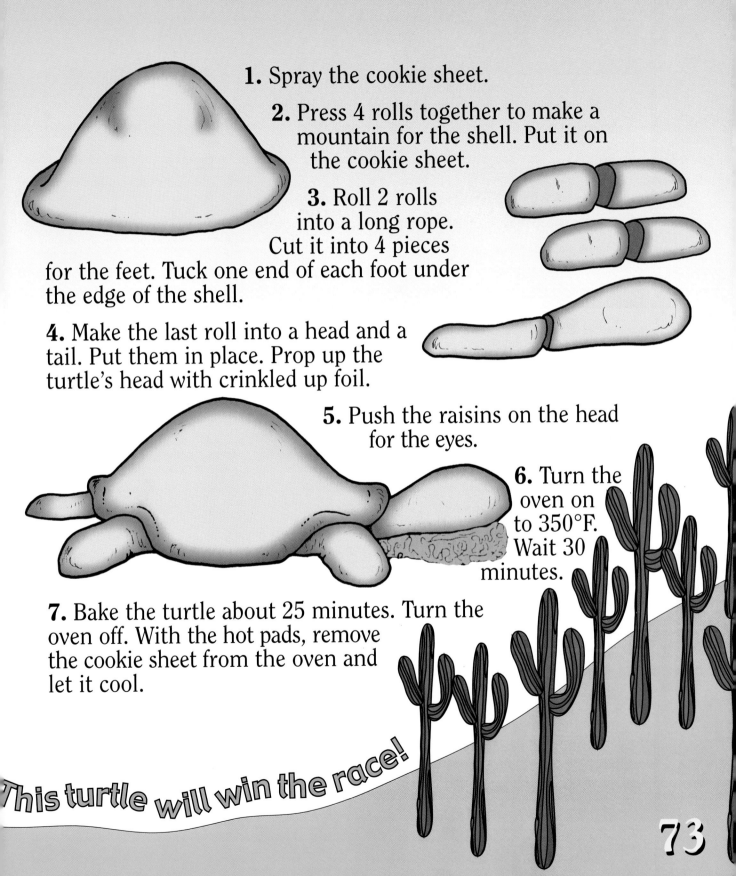

1. Spray the cookie sheet.

2. Press 4 rolls together to make a mountain for the shell. Put it on the cookie sheet.

3. Roll 2 rolls into a long rope. Cut it into 4 pieces for the feet. Tuck one end of each foot under the edge of the shell.

4. Make the last roll into a head and a tail. Put them in place. Prop up the turtle's head with crinkled up foil.

5. Push the raisins on the head for the eyes.

6. Turn the oven on to 350°F. Wait 30 minutes.

7. Bake the turtle about 25 minutes. Turn the oven off. With the hot pads, remove the cookie sheet from the oven and let it cool.

This turtle will win the race!

Dough Writing

Equipment
cookie sheet
non-stick cooking spray
scissors
hot pads

Ingredients
8 Rhodes Texas™ rolls

Advance Preparation
Put the frozen rolls in a plastic bag. Leave them in the refrigerator overnight or on the counter for about 2 hours, until thawed but still cold.

1. Spray the cookie sheet.

2. Roll each roll into a long rope.

3. Cut and pinch the dough to make the letters or numbers. Put them on the cookie sheet—not too close together!

4. Turn the oven on to 350°F. Wait 15 minutes.

5. Bake the writing about 20 minutes. Turn the oven off. With the hot pads, remove the cookie sheet from the oven and let it cool.

Piggy

Equipment
cookie sheet
non-stick
   cooking spray
knife
pencil
hot pads

oink! oink! oink!

Ingredients
4 Rhodes Texas™ rolls
2 raisins

Advance Preparation
Put the frozen rolls in a plastic bag. Leave them in the refrigerator overnight or on the counter for about 2 hours, until thawed but still cold.

1. Spray the cookie sheet.

2. Flatten 2 rolls together for the head. Put it on the cookie sheet.

3. Cut 1 roll in half. Use one half to make 2 feet. Put them under the head.

4. With the other half make a nose and a tail. Poke holes in the nose with the end of a pencil. Put the nose and tail on the pig.

5. Flatten the last roll into a rectangle. Cut it in half for the ears. Put them on the head and fold them over.

6. Push the raisins on the head for the eyes. Turn the oven on to 350°F. Wait 20 minutes.

7. Just before baking, poke the nose holes again. Bake the piggy about 20 minutes. Turn the oven off. With the hot pads, remove the cookie sheet from the oven and let it cool.

This little piggy stayed home!

A^x Apples

Equipment
cookie sheet
non-stick cooking spray
knife
hot pads

Ingredients
2 Rhodes Texas™ rolls

Advance Preparation
Put the frozen rolls in a plastic bag. Leave them in the refrigerator overnight or on the counter for about 2 hours, until thawed but still cold.

78

1. Spray the cookie sheet.

2. Flatten 2 rolls together for the apple. Put it on the cookie sheet.

3. Cut triangles out of the apple.

4. Make a small piece of leftover dough into a stem. Put it at the top of the apple.

5. Flatten the remaining dough into a leaf. Cut the vein. Put the leaf next to the stem.

6. Turn the oven on to 350°F. Wait 20 minutes.

7. Bake the apple about 20 minutes. Turn the oven off. With the hot pads, remove the cookie sheet from the oven and let it cool.

An apple a day o o o

Breadsticks

Equipment
9 x 13-inch pan
2 small bowls
plastic wrap
hot pads

Ingredients
8 Rhodes Texas™ rolls
1/4 cup butter
1/4 cup Parmesan cheese
garlic salt or
    McCormick/Schilling Salad
    Supreme® seasoning, if desired

Advance Preparation
Put the frozen rolls in a plastic bag. Leave them in the refrigerator overnight or on the counter for about 2 hours, until thawed but still cold.

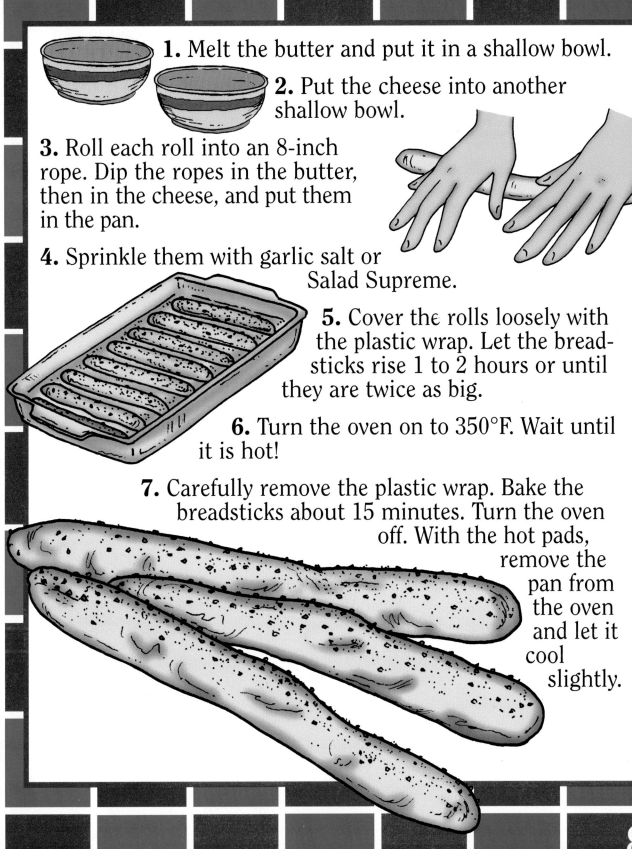

1. Melt the butter and put it in a shallow bowl.

2. Put the cheese into another shallow bowl.

3. Roll each roll into an 8-inch rope. Dip the ropes in the butter, then in the cheese, and put them in the pan.

4. Sprinkle them with garlic salt or Salad Supreme.

5. Cover the rolls loosely with the plastic wrap. Let the bread-sticks rise 1 to 2 hours or until they are twice as big.

6. Turn the oven on to 350°F. Wait until it is hot!

7. Carefully remove the plastic wrap. Bake the breadsticks about 15 minutes. Turn the oven off. With the hot pads, remove the pan from the oven and let it cool slightly.

81

Autumn Leaves

Equipment
paper and pencil
scissors
cookie sheet
non-stick cooking spray
knife
hot pads

Ingredients
2 or 3 Rhodes Texas™ rolls

Advance Preparation
Put the frozen rolls in a plastic bag. Leave them in the refrigerator overnight or on the counter for about 2 hours, until thawed but still cold.

1. Photocopy or trace the leaf patterns on this page onto a piece of paper, or draw some of your own. Cut them out.

2. Spray the cookie sheet.

3. Flatten the rolls together into a circle. Put the pattern on the dough and cut the leaf out. Put it on the cookie sheet.

4. Cut veins on the leaf.

5. With a piece of the leftover dough, make a stem. Put it at the bottom of the leaf.

6. Turn the oven on to 350°F. Wait 20 minutes.

7. Bake the leaf about 20 minutes. Turn the oven off. With the hot pads, remove the cookie sheet from the oven and let it cool.

Get out the rake!

Curly Dogs

Equipment
cookie sheet
non-stick cooking spray
hot pads

Ingredients
8 Rhodes Texas™ rolls
1 package hot dogs
ketchup
mustard

Advance Preparation
Put the frozen rolls in a plastic bag. Leave them in the refrigerator overnight or on the counter for about 2 hours, until thawed but still cold.

1. Spray the cookie sheet.

2. Roll each roll into a rope.

3. Twist the rope around each hot dog and tuck the ends under the dough. Put them on the cookie sheet.

4. Turn the oven on to 350°F. Wait 30 minutes.

5. Bake the curly dogs about 20 minutes. Turn the oven off. With the hot pads, remove the cookie sheet from the oven and let it cool slightly. Serve the curly dogs warm with ketchup and mustard.

These curly dogs may also be cooked over hot coals at a summet cookout!

Hallowieners:

1. Spray the cookie sheet. Turn the oven on to 350°F.

2. Roll a long rope and decorate it for the snake's body.

3. On the larger end of the snake, poke holes for the nose and cut a slash for the mouth.

4. Crinkle up a small piece of aluminum foil and put it in the mouth to hold it open during baking.

5. Wrap the snake body around a hot dog. Put it on the cookie sheet.

6. Poke deep holes for the eyes and press raisins in them.

7. Bake the hallowieners about 20 minutes. Turn the oven off. Using the hot pads, remove the cookie sheet from the oven and let it cool.

8. Stick a short piece of licorice into the throat and clip the end for a forked tongue.

Spooky Spider

Equipment
cookie sheet
non-stick cooking spray
knife
hot pads

Ingredients
2 loaves Rhodes™ bread dough
2 raisins

Don't get caught in the web!

COOKING SPRAY

Advance Preparation
Put the frozen loaves in a plastic bag. Leave them in the refrigerator overnight or on the counter for about 3 hours, until thawed but still cold.

1. Spray the cookie sheet.

2. Make 1 loaf into a ball for the body. Put it on the cookie sheet.

3. Cut a small piece off the other loaf for the head. Make it into a ball and put it next to the body.

4. Slice the rest of the loaf into 8 strips for the legs. Roll them into ropes and put them in place.

5. Push the raisins on the head for the eyes.

6. Turn the oven on to 350°F. Wait 30 minutes.

7. Bake the spider about 25 minutes. Turn the oven off. With the hot pads, remove the cookie sheet from the oven and let it cool.

For a spooky dip bowl, hollow out my stomach and fill me with dip or nacho cheese sauce. Serve with veggies or chips!

Ghost

Equipment
cookie sheet
non-stick cooking spray
scissors
pencil with a clean eraser
hot pads

Ingredients
3 Rhodes Texas™ rolls

Advance Preparation
Put the frozen rolls in a plastic bag. Leave them in the refrigerator overnight or on the counter for about 2 hours, until thawed but still cold.

1. Spray the cookie sheet.

2. Flatten the rolls together to make the ghost. Put it on the cookie sheet.

3. Make cuts for the arms.

4. Pull the arms down, and the bottom to one side.

5. Poke and stretch big holes for the eyes and the mouth.

6. Turn the oven on to 350°F. Wait 20 minutes.

7. Poke the holes for the eyes and the mouth again. Bake the ghost about 20 minutes. Turn the oven off. With the hot pads, remove the cookie sheet from the oven and let it cool.

Boo!

Curly Dogs
recipe on pages 84 & 85

Witch's Cat
recipe on pages 92 & 93

Barney the Bat
recipe on pages 94 & 95

Witch's Cat

Equipment
cookie sheet
non-stick cooking spray
scissors
knife
hot pads

Ingredients
4 Rhodes Texas™ rolls
1 currant

Advance Preparation
Put the frozen rolls in a plastic bag. Leave them in the refrigerator overnight or on the counter for about 2 hours, until thawed but still cold.

1. Spray the cookie sheet.

2. Squish 2 rolls together and roll them into a rope for the body and legs. Bend it in half and put it on the cookie sheet.

3. Make a cut on each side for the legs and pull them apart.

4. Roll 1 roll into the tail. Put it by the body.

5. Flatten the last roll into a circle for the cat's head. Cut a piece out of the top. Put the head above the cat's body.

6. With some leftover dough make 3 balls for the mouth. Put them on the face. Push a currant above the mouth for the nose. Cut slits for the eyes.

7. Clip the fur.

8. Turn the oven on to 350°F. Wait 20 minutes.

9. Bake the cat about 20 minutes. Turn the oven off. With the hot pads, remove the cookie sheet from the oven and let it cool.

Meow!

Barney the Bat

Equipment
cookie sheet
non-stick cooking spray
knife
hot pads

Ingredients
4 Rhodes Texas™ rolls
2 currants

Advance Preparation
Put the frozen rolls in a plastic bag. Leave them in the refrigerator overnight or on the counter for about 2 hours, until thawed but still cold.

94

1. Spray the cookie sheet.

2. Flatten 1 roll for the bat's body. Cut out a triangle. Put the body on the cookie sheet.

3. Flatten 2 rolls into 2 triangles for the wings. Put them by the body. Cut triangles out of each wing.

4. Cut lines in the wings and pinch the tops together.

5. Cut 1 roll in half and flatten one half for the head. Make a cut and pull the ears apart. Put the head above the body. Press your finger deep into each ear.

6. Use the last half for the bat's feet. Cut the toes. Put them below the bat.

7. With some leftover dough, make 3 balls for the mouth. Put them in place. Push the currants on the face for the eyes and nose.

8. Turn the oven on to 350°F. Wait 20 minutes.

9. Press your finger into each ear again. Bake the bat about 20 minutes. Turn the oven off. With the hot pads, remove the cookie sheet from the oven and let it cool.

Cinnamon Rolls

Equipment
cookie sheet
non-stick cooking spray
plastic wrap
knife
hot pads

Ingredients
12 Rhodes™ cinnamon rolls

Advance Preparation
This recipe uses dough that is still frozen. After step 3, they can be put in the refrigerator overnight to thaw. Then let them rise 2 hours on the counter before following step 5.

1. Spray the cookie sheet.

2. Put the cinnamon rolls on the cookie sheet.

3. Spray the plastic wrap and cover the rolls loosely.

4. Let the cinnamon rolls rise about 4 hours or until they are twice as big.

5. Turn the oven on to 350°F. Wait until it is hot!

6. Carefully remove the plastic wrap. Bake the cinnamon rolls about 15 to 20 minutes or until they are light golden brown.

7. Turn the oven off. With the hot pads, remove the cookie sheet from the oven and let it cool slightly.

8. Frost the cinnamon rolls while they are still warm.

oooey! gooey!

Really Good Rolls

Equipment

8-inch square baking pan
non-stick cooking spray
plastic wrap
hot pads

Ingredients

9 Rhodes Texas™ rolls
butter
jam

Advance Preparation

This recipe uses dough that is still frozen. After step 3, they can be put in the refrigerator overnight to thaw. Then let them rise 2 hours on the counter before following step 5.

1. Spray the square baking pan.

2. Put the rolls in the pan.

3. Spray the plastic wrap and cover the rolls loosely.

4. Let the rolls rise about 4 hours or until they are twice as big.

5. Turn the oven on to 350°F. Wait until it is hot!

6. Carefully remove the plastic wrap. Bake the rolls 15 to 20 minutes or until they are light golden brown.

7. Turn the oven off. With the hot pads, remove the pan from the oven. Tip the rolls out and let them cool slightly. Serve them warm with butter and jam.

Butter me up!

Texas Turkey

Equipment
cookie sheet
non-stick cooking spray
scissors
fork
small bowl
pastry brush
hot pads

Gobble me up!

Ingredients
2 Rhodes Texas™ rolls
1 egg
1 peppercorn (for the eye)
1 slivered almond (for the beak)
nuts and seeds
pretzel sticks

Advance Preparation
Put the frozen rolls in a plastic bag. Leave them in the refrigerator overnight or on the counter for about 2 hours, until thawed but still cold.

1. Spray the cookie sheet.

2. Flatten 1 roll for the turkey's body. Put it on the cookie sheet.

3. Cut a small piece off the other roll and make it into the head and neck. Cut the wattle. Put it by the neck.

4. Flatten the rest of the roll into a half circle and cut the feathers. Put it next to the turkey.

5. Beat the egg and brush it on the turkey. Push the eye and beak on the face. Decorate your turkey with the nuts and seeds.

6. Turn the oven on to 350°F. Wait 20 minutes.

7. Bake the turkey about 20 minutes. Turn the oven off. With the hot pads, remove the cookie sheet from the oven and let it cool. Use pretzels for the legs.

101

Honey Bear

Equipment
cookie sheet
non-stick cooking spray
scissors
hot pads

Ingredients
7 Rhodes Texas™ rolls

Advance Preparation
Put the frozen rolls in a plastic bag. Leave them in the refrigerator overnight or on the counter for about 2 hours, until thawed but still cold.

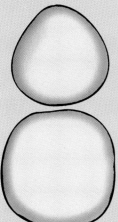

1. Spray the cookie sheet.

2. Flatten 3 rolls together for the body. Put it on the cookie sheet.

3. Flatten 2 rolls together for the head. Put it above the body.

4. Cut one roll in half. Roll one half into a ball for the muzzle. Put it on the face.

5. Use the other half to make the eyes, ears, nose and belly button. Put them in place.

6. Make the last roll into 2 small paws and 2 big feet. Put them on the sides of the bear.

7. Turn the oven on to 350°F. Wait 20 minutes.

8. Bake the bear about 20 minutes. Turn the oven off. With the hot pads, remove the cookie sheet from the oven and let it cool.

GRRR!!!

Maddie Mouse

Equipment
cookie sheet
non-stick cooking spray
scissors
hot pads

Ingredients
2 Rhodes Texas™ rolls
2 small raisins

Advance Preparation
Put the frozen rolls in a plastic bag. Leave them in the refrigerator overnight or on the counter for about 2 hours, until thawed but still cold.

1. Spray the cookie sheet.

2. Flatten 1 roll into the mouse's body. Put it on the cookie sheet.

3. Cut the other roll into 3 pieces. Make 1 piece into a flat circle for the mouse's leg. Put it on the body.

4. Cut the second piece in half and make 2 ears. Put them above the head. Press your finger deep into the middle of each ear.

5. Make the last piece into a tail, a foot and a hand. Cut the fingers. Put them all in place.

6. Push the raisins on the mouse for the eye and the nose.

7. Turn the oven on to 350°F. Wait 20 minutes.

8. Bake the mouse about 20 minutes. Turn the oven off. With the hot pads, remove the cookie sheet from the oven and let it cool.

Squeak! Squeak!

Moose

Hang me on the wall.

Equipment
cookie sheet
non-stick cooking spray
rolling pin
knife
scissors
hot pads

Ingredients
2 loaves Rhodes™ bread dough
1 raisin

Advance Preparation
Put the frozen loaves in a plastic bag. Leave them in the refrigerator overnight or on the counter for about 3 hours, until thawed but still cold.

1. Spray the cookie sheet.

2. Flatten 1 loaf into a moose head. Put it on the cookie sheet. Cut the mouth and shaggy chin hairs.

3. Cut the other loaf in half. Flatten and cut 1 half for the antlers. Put them above the head.

4. Make an ear with some of the leftover dough. Fold it in half and put it on the head.

5. Flatten the last half of the loaf for the neck. Put it under the chin.

6. Push a raisin on the head for the eye.

7. Turn the oven on to 350°F. Wait 30 minutes.

8. Just before baking, press your thumb deep into the face to make the nostril. Bake the moose about 25 minutes. Turn the oven off. With the hot pads, remove the cookie sheet from the oven and let it cool.

107

Tall Timbers

Equipment
cookie sheet
non-stick cooking spray
knife
hot pads

Ingredients
2 Rhodes Texas™ rolls

Advance Preparation
Put the frozen rolls in a plastic bag.
Leave them in the refrigerator
overnight or on the counter for about
2 hours, until thawed but still cold.

1. Spray the cookie sheet.

2. Flatten the rolls together into a tall thin triangle for the tree. Put it on the cookie sheet.

3. Cut a piece off the bottom for the trunk. Put it beneath the tree.

4. Make cuts on each side of the triangle and pull out the branches. Stretch the tree to make it taller.

5. Turn the oven on to 350°F. Wait 20 minutes.

6. Bake the tall timber about 20 minutes. Turn the oven off. With the hot pads, remove the cookie sheet from the oven and let it cool.

Timber!

For Parents

Equivalents for Frozen Dough

1 loaf of Rhodes™ frozen bread dough (16 oz.) = 8 Rhodes Texas™ Rolls or 12 Rhodes™ rolls

Frozen Dough Tips

How to Buy

Rhodes products are located in the frozen food section of your grocery store. When purchasing Rhodes dough check the package for these things:

- For a fresher product, buy dough with an expiration date of several months away (found on the package or closure tab.)
- Rolls or loaves should be separate, not frozen together.
- Dough should be frozen solid with no ice crystals or frost in the package.

How to Thaw

Always cover dough while thawing.

- Allow 8 hours in a refrigerator or 2 to 3 hours at room temperature. Thawed dough can be refrigerated for up to 2 days but will continue to rise.
- Do not re-freeze thawed dough. (Rhodes frozen dough may be frozen after it is baked and cooled.)

How to Rise

All Rhodes products should double in size before they are ready to bake (except for dough sculpture.)

- To keep dough soft and moist while rising, always cover with plastic wrap sprayed with non-stick cooking spray.
- Dough will rise faster in a warm, moist area. Do not let the dough over-rise.

How to Bake

Dough is ready to bake when finger pushes dough and an indentation remains.

- Remove the plastic wrap carefully before baking.
- Bake Rhodes products according to directions on package or follow recipe instructions.
- Bread should have a rich golden brown color when baked.
- Bake on the middle rack for best results.

Dough Sculpture Helps

- Using wheat dough will add character to your scultpure. It also holds its shape better when sculpting and is easier to work with.

- Brush the sculpture with a beaten egg before baking to make it shiny or when decorating your sculpture with nuts, seeds, etc.

- Scissors work great for cutting the dough. Supervise children when using a knife or scissors.

- The wait time on the dough sculpture recipes is to allow the oven to heat and the dough to rise.

For Kids

MAZE

Can you find your way through the maze to the hot pizza below?

WHEEL OF WORDS

Starting at the pointer and going in a clockwise direction, write every other letter in the spaces beside the wheel.

(Skip 2 spaces after the letter "H")

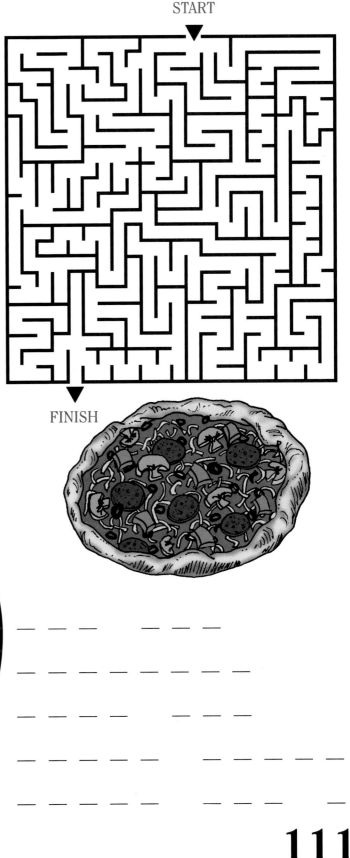

START

FINISH

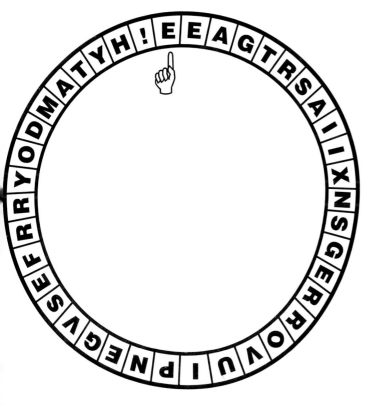

__ __ __ __

__ __ __ __

__ __ __

__ __ __ __

__ __ __ __

111

Great Savings from Rhodes™!

Save $2
on any package of Rhodes™ frozen dough

In your grocer's freezer

Expires 12/31/2015   Manufacturer's Coupon   40084-3

5 70022 50082 1   (8100) 0 40084

Save $1
on any package of Rhodes™ frozen dough

In your grocer's freezer

Expires 12/31/2015   Manufacturer's Coupon   40085-0

5 70022 50076 0   (8100) 0 40085

Save 50¢
on any package of Rhodes™ frozen dough

In your grocer's freezer

Expires 12/31/2015   Manufacturer's Coupon   40086-8

5 70022 50050 0   (8100) 0 40086

Save 50¢
on any package of Rhodes™ frozen dough

In your grocer's freezer

Expires 12/31/2015   Manufacturer's Coupon   40087-6

5 70022 50050 0   (8100) 0 40087